MICROCOSM · PUBLISHING

Microcosm Publishing is Portland's most diversified publishing house and distributor with a focus on the colorful, authentic, and empowering. Our books and zines have put your power in your hands since 1996, equipping readers to make positive changes in their lives and in the world around them. Microcosm emphasizes skill-building, showing hidden histories, and fostering creativity through challenging conventional publishing wisdom with books and bookettes about DIY skills, food, bicycling, gender, self-care, and social justice. What was once a distro and record label was started by Joe Biel in his bedroom and has become among the oldest independent publishing houses in Portland, OR. We are a politically moderate, centrist publisher in a world that has inched to the right for the past 80 years.

I've always wanted to write a book. Since as far back as I can remember, I have been intrigued by the thought of laying down my own story. In the following pages, I will have by no means even scratched the surface of that book, but my hope is to at least share one meaningful chapter of it. Maybe you can relate a little, maybe you can even learn something from my mistakes and discoveries. In honestly reflecting on my wrongdoings and challenging myself to share the story of my own struggle through the darkness, perhaps I can inspire someone else to fight through theirs. If this small part of my journey can somehow help to guide even one person in the right direction, then all of my hard work in trying to do the right thing will have paid off. Take it or leave it, but know that it is my truth. It all starts with a simple question. . . "Why am I in prison?"

• • •

Here I am in prison in the middle-of-nowhere Ohio. Even though I am over three years into serving a 3–4 year sentence, I still have a hard time figuring out exactly how I ended up here. Maybe, even still, I just don't want to believe it. I've lost just about everything in my life, save for the family and friends that have somehow stuck by me on this journey. The only material possessions I have fit into a 2.4-cubic-foot metal box and on two wooden coat hooks, half of that belonging to the State anyway. I can only speak to the family that supports me from thousands of miles away through monitored, interrupted, 15 minute phone calls about once a week, if I'm lucky. My life consists of concrete, metal, bad meals, waiting in line for absolutely everything, everyday, and being told when or where I am able to do even the most basic things, like using the bathroom. I haven't even seen the stars in 3 years.

Although I'm lost as a statistic amongst this sea of numbers right now, I can gladly say that I've been able to find myself again. Most people call me Goldsby. I am inmate #A735694. Although I am proud of my Goldsby name, no nickname or inmate number describes who I really am. The truth is, despite my sentence (four years for 2nd degree burglary, if you're wondering), I like to think of myself as a decent human being. You can call me Devan. It's nice to meet you

Despite evidence to the contrary, lying, stealing, and manipulation are not parts of my true character. I can't take all of my past actions back, as much as I wish that I could. The inner struggle between the light and dark in this human experience can get overwhelming, to say the least. With no knowledge or guidance in how to make sense of it all, or any idea of how to cope with shit experiences, it's easy for us to either get tunnel vision or to completely lose focus altogether. I consider myself to be an honest, respectful, and good-hearted person that believes in loyalty and integrity.

So it really baffles me to reflect on the Devan that I've shown to other people at times. Was it really me that lied, manipulated, stole, and took advantage of people? Was it really me that broke people's trust and people's hearts? Even the very people that are dearest to me, the ones that I love and care about more than anything. How could I be the one to completely destroy everything that was good and beautiful in my life? Is that really me? Is that the Devan I have become?

• • •

The story that led me to this point in my life is long and winding. I do intend to share that with the world in more detail someday, but that will be saved for "The Book." In order for this to make sense, however, I do have to try to briefly explain some of it. Without a past, there wouldn't be much to grow from, would there? How could we measure failure or success without having some sort of point to hook the tape measure to and start pulling? Well, here we go.

I grew up on the Flathead Indian Reservation in Northwestern Montana. Growing up on the Rez was unique, to say the least. It is an open reservation, meaning that the Cowboys and the Natives all share the same land. This meeting of cultures provided a different kind of community and most of the time I felt like the minority, being a white boy, or *suyapi*, in Salish. Despite being an outsider, I found a more accepting environment in native culture and I chose to be around them more often than not.

The Rez is the most beautiful place that I've ever been. I had the Rocky Mountains as my backyard. I valued learning the customs and traditions from the local people. We didn't have water parks or malls with arcades but what we did have was freshwater lakes and rivers, abundant wildlife, close knit communities, farms, endless back roads, and a true connection to the land.

I took the initiative to learn as much as I could about the old ways from the Elders. I learned how to bead and create traditional artwork, how to survive in the wild, and even how to speak some of the Salish language. I also spent some wonderful summers living in a tipi and had the privilege to sit in a few drum circles.

Now, while I was growing up in the most beautiful place on Earth, it all came with a hidden cost. The Rez seemed to have a perpetual dark cloud hovering over it. There was always this elusive negativity and evil lingering in the shadows of its beauty. If you didn't learn to acknowledge and respect this cloud's presence, it would eventually force itself into your life even more. There was no ignoring it, and absolutely no fighting against it. One had no choice but to figure out how to live with it and find some kind of balance.

I found that the more it seemed things were going well, the closer disaster was to striking. I know that I'm not the only person to notice this. It is tied to the land and it radiates through all aspects of your life. It's a land, both literally and figuratively, of idyllic sunsets and waterfalls with rainbows in the mist, but with that beauty comes the jagged cliffs and untamed wild that can lead to tragedy at any moment.

The Rez showed me how to be fearless, enticing me into adventures and near death experiences. I don't know if it was a guardian angel, luck, or if I was just destined to live more life, but I somehow made it out and I began to believe that I could escape the dark cloud's grasp. I managed to seek out positive things in my life. I played sports, I sang in the choir. I would go fishing, hiking, camping, riding my bicycle everywhere, and even had the opportunity to travel. I picked up art, photography, and tried to play the guitar. Driving became an outlet too. Just being able to cruise around aimlessly and smoke was such an amazing feeling of freedom.

My favorite by far, and still to this day, however, is skateboarding. Skating has always been the one thing in my life that would consistently light up the darkness. The comradery that is ingrained in skateboarding communities, and the thrill of pushing each other to new levels is incredible. The energy created from a bunch of skate heads tearing up a spot is so exhilarating. Even just navigating the concrete waves and terrain alone on my board is one of the greatest feelings ever.

I managed to learn a lot about myself growing up in the chaos of the Rez. I grew to be strong and closed off. My heart learned how to go numb and ice over for protection, but not before it was stomped on a few times. My father left my life when I was about three years old and the only male figure that I ever allowed to replace him thereafter was my grandfather. He was my number one role model. Aside from periodic guidance from my uncle and other men who came in and out of my life, Grandpa was the one. He taught me most everything that built the foundation for my character today. Not only did I inherit his name and his baldness, but also his work ethic, stubbornness, charm, drive, and big heart. I also learned from his explosive temper how to remain calm. Overall, he did his best to teach me how to be a man and how to navigate my own path through this life.

My mother has many of her own unique traits that were handed down to me as well. She taught me how to be respectful, kind, honest, and loving. Among the many things she passed on to me, however, some were a bit more problematic. Notably, how to drown my feelings and avoid confronting my problems. She struggled with alcohol, and for the longest time I couldn't understand it. I would watch her drink away her feelings and her pain and I learned by misexample how not to go about coping with life's hard times. Despite this, I am proud to say that she is doing great nowadays.

As my brother and I grew up as a couple of white boys on the Rez, we stayed close for a long time. His perspective may be a little different than my own, but I'd like to think that I was a good big brother to him, at least when I was there. There were six years between us, so I was put in the position of caretaker and teacher as well as brother. Eventually the Rez exploited that age gap, however, and started to draw us apart.

Looking back on our childhood, I have realized that it was actually him who taught me some things. I felt like some of my childhood was robbed because I had to step up at such a young age to not only be a brother, but a father figure as well. Both good and bad came from this experience. The good was that he taught me responsibility, maturity, compassion, empathy, and especially patience. On the other hand, I had the perfect excuse to rebel against responsibility and maturity later on in life. I already had to be the adult, so I felt I deserved the chance to be the selfish kid again. Right?

• • •

The roots of my failures in life seem to have been grown in a dark garden of tragedy, numbness, fear of potential, and a love of chaos. Somewhere along the way, I must have unintentionally tended too much to this side of myself. Perhaps in trying to care for my inner light, I managed to inadvertently nourish this dark garden. All in all, my experiences on the Rez chiseled me straight out of the solid Rocky Mountains. I came through it all with a few insecurities and character flaws, but I could still see the silver lining in life.

The biggest and darkest seeds planted in that garden of misery and chaos, were sown by death. No matter how fearless of death I was myself, I could never understand it when it happened around me. It started to seem as if my curse was to live a long life, enduring the pain of death other than my own. People were dying from overdose, car wrecks, accidental drownings, and freak accidents.It started out as acquaintances or friends of friends, and even distant family members. But death soon moved in closer and closer. We all lost close friends and family during our later years in high school that devastated everyone. On more than one occasion, I should have been in a fatal crash with friends that were lost, but somehow my life was spared.

My mom always said that I have guardian angels. The hardest part about going through all of this boiled down to not knowing how to cope. They don't teach us how to go about things like that in school. So, not knowing any other way, we all turned to just trying to numb it all out. I didn't do this consciously, but I couldn't fix the problems so I just tried to sweep them under the rug. Perhaps I learned more from my mother than I thought.

After a few years of confusion, chaos, and emotional isolation, the garden within was suddenly provided with enough fertilizer to overgrow and block out even the brightest of lights. My closest and best friend since kindergarten, Brice, died in a tragic car wreck within a couple hours of dropping me off at home. It is at this point in my life that I finally just snapped. I allowed the darkness to overgrow in my heart, and my attitude switched to fuck-it mode.

Before Brice died, my drug and alcohol use was a completely different story. I had smoked marijuana since the very young age of 12 years old. It never felt like it was a problem for me and many of my friends did the same thing. I smoked on occasion, but would quit for basketball and tennis seasons. I did eventually get into some minor trouble once or twice with it, but only for the simple fact that it was illegal. Weed didn't fry my brain or make me do anything crazy like jump off a cliff or try to rob somebody to get more. I still graduated from high school with an Honors Diploma and always continued to work towards my dreams and goals. The marijuana just helped me open up new thought waves to understand and make sense of the world in a different light. I would use it socially to have some good times and good laughs with friends. I would also smoke by myself to either relax and enjoy some music, or even to spark some creative thoughts for motivation to work on a project. Weed had become a normal part of my life and my own personal religion so to speak. It felt harmless.

The alcohol, of course, was a little more dangerous. I knew the potential danger for major problems caused by alcohol, so I did try to approach it with caution. I learned by misexample what not to do, so I tried my best to drink responsibly. Unfortunately though, I could handle my alcohol. This led to bigger problems, like always being trusted and elected to be the D.D.D. (Designated Drunk Driver). I definitely made some poor decisions in my drinking, but I didn't drink all of the time. It was more of a social thing, if not just because we were all bored with very few things to do on the Rez. It wasn't like I was always trying to get shitfaced. I just wanted to switch it up to have some different fun here and there.

I experimented with other drugs, more or less out of curiosity rather than peer pressure. I went on some much needed magical mushroom journeys that really helped me figure out my place in life. I snorted or ate some pain pills a couple of times, but wasn't really drawn into it. I even tried snorting meth once, almost out of spite for all of the anti-meth ads that read, "Meth, not even once." It was the worst thing ever, and I immediately regretted it. Along with tobacco, I had become the biggest anti-meth advocate thereafter. Whether or not I may have had access to try other drugs on the Rez, I chose not to. I would never let my curiosity get out of hand, because I knew better. I was glad to have discovered mushrooms, because in using them as a spiritual means to reground and even find myself, I had grown tremendously as a person. Nothing else really appealed to me, and so I stuck to the comfort of my weed, alcohol, poppy seed muffins, and chai tea lattes.

In college, however, I decided to become more adventurous. I started drinking more, mostly because I really loved beer pong. The whole social aspect of drinking in college was fun, not to mention that I could buy alcohol at the age of 18 because I was already balding and never got carded. I was still the "responsible" one that everybody trusted. I tried a few more drugs, red rock opium, hash, cocaine, some different kinds of pills like adderall or xanax, and way better weed. The one that I enjoyed the most, however, was ecstacy. I started experimenting with mixing drugs for different highs. Some 'shrooms and ecstasy with a little weed was one of the best nights of my life. Overall though, I wasn't some out of control junkie that partied all day every day. I was disciplined enough to only be a weekend warrior and not let any of it affect my schooling, for the most part. I was only having a good time, and I never did anything crazy to try to get high. If I didn't have it, no big deal.

After college, and living back on the Rez again, however, it turned into a different story. I wish that I could say that there was some long foreseen slow decline into my addiction and that it was all so obvious that surely I could have gotten help sooner. That was never the case. I was always in control before, so nobody ever realized that there was ever a potential problem. I was always the good boy that had his head on straight and everyone looked up to me. But then Brice died.

Most people who experience trauma, like death, explain how they drank or used to numb out the pain. Even I thought that's what I was doing for years. What I've discovered is that I didn't spiral into alcoholism and using absolutely everything in my path in order to numb the pain. I did it in order to feel. I was so devastated by his loss that I was utterly shattered. I went so numb that I lost all emotion. I couldn't even cry to mourn his death and people noticed. After failing to be able to express my grief over Brice's death in front of hundreds of people at his wake service, I became socially withdrawn. I didn't know how to act anymore, or what to do with my life. So I drank. I started smoking cigarettes. I did everything that I could to feel something, to feel anything at all.

I became a really cold person thereafter. People knew that I had a good heart, so they were blind to what I was becoming. I was always the solid rock. Nobody expected me to crumble inside. Eventually, some people began to notice the difference in me. They started to see the pain inside that I couldn't cope with and they were drawn to it out of either a desire to help or maybe because they could relate in some way. I was very thankful to have their concern, and so I indulged in seeking those normal relationships. The thing about it was that, even though I seemed to be somewhat functioning on the outside, nobody could see that such a big part of me had died on the inside, and neither could I.

While trying to embrace any kind of love or friendship, I began to subconsciously hurt a lot of people around me that I loved. I was used to sharing the goodness of my heart, but I didn't realize that I was inadvertently spreading poison around from my damaged inner self. My desire for love to fill the void had become a bug zapper, leading many into this harmful, artificial light. I'm sorry for the people that I hurt during my struggles with grief. I know that it's not okay, and it never will be, but I hope that they can all understand and possibly even forgive me someday.

I went off the deep end for some time, but I was eventually saved by my uncle before it was too late. He took me away from the dark cloud of the Rez and gave me an amazing opportunity to start fresh. I was skeptical to take off in a beat-up, old '77 Dodge motorhome, but I was ready to get away. I was trying to sweep the past under the rug and distract myself with adventure in order to find myself again for a while. I got to see the country, rediscover who I was, and even remember what my journey was about again.

I worked miscellaneous jobs. Everything from joining a traveling carnival, maintaining major roadways for the Ecology Department, and even apprenticing to learn the trades of custom formica countertops and vinyl flooring. I was even able to indulge in my skills of creating art and restoring old furniture. I had gotten out of my slump for the most part, and I was able to work, skate, and live. I even proved my own potential by going to LA on my own and actually finding some success. It was to be a short trip to visit a friend, but it turned into a substantial part of my life where I was self-sufficient and felt on top of the world.

After being uprooted from my dark garden, I managed to return to skating. I was able to skate my brains out in every place I went. The lifestyle of surfing any rollable terrain on my four wheels and not having any other care or worry in the world was such a valuable release. I could show up to any skatepark from Washington State all the way down to San Diego and be blessed with built-in, like-minded friends. I had the comradery of random strangers who came together in those places with the same goal: skate or die.

So I was able to skate my way back into feeling again. I was alive. Whether having some witnesses at the park to verify the phat backside heel on the hip, or throwing down the sickest line all alone on the streets, working magic on my skateboard was always the best feeling. I would gladly accept a thousand bad days skating than even one day without it. Although the drinking and smoking continued, being hand in hand with the skateboarder's lifestyle, I was back to only using for the right reasons. I was functioning and I was happy.

• • •

Eventually I found myself back at the farmhouse in Battle Ground, Washington. Being a hop, skip, and a switch flip away from Portland, Oregon was ideal. The people around were generally alright and I had access to tons of skateboarding. Between the naked bicycle rides of Portland, the wildlife close at hand, lots to do for work, and access to the Gorge and the breathtaking volcanoes of the area, I was comfortable there. As opposed to the horrid gravel or dirt backroads of Montana, all the backroads of Battle Ground were mostly paved, making for smooth adventures into the wild. I really enjoyed it there, and it was a nice reprieve from the overcrowded chaos of Los Angeles. I felt that it was a really good balance between L.A. and back home on the Rez, minus that dark cloud. I was content.

This is where I met Nikki. She had come out from Ohio to visit her mother and ended up staying. She was fun, outgoing, smart, kind, thoughtful, adventurous, and of course, beautiful. I was at a place in my life where I was confident in myself after conquering L.A., and I knew that was attractive to Nikki. She could somehow see the good in my heart.

Unfortunately for her sake, she was oblivious of the dark garden hidden within me. We started to have fun together, and became more than good friends very quickly. I didn't want a serious relationship, but I had a problem with assertive communication at times and actually expressing that. I was always open minded to giving things a chance, however. She fell in love with me very quickly, and I, being a hopeless romantic and trying to make her happy didn't help that one bit. I enjoyed the way that she made me feel wanted and appreciated. It was a very comfortable and attractive situation, so I indulged.

We lived together in love and contentment for a year before we got pregnant. She didn't get pregnant, we did. After this, things began to change. As much as I had never wanted to bring an innocent life into the chaos of this world, the decision was beyond me now. I was scared shitless at first, knowing that the rest of my life was changed forever, but I would always do the right thing and stand by my girls' side. My father had abandoned me, and that was absolutely against all that I believed in and stood for. I would always be there for my girls no matter what, nothing could ever change that, or so I thought.

Something about the whole situation must have triggered that garden inside me to slowly bloom again. I don't know if I was scared because I didn't want that responsibility to not hurt someone, or because I knew that I wouldn't be free to roam the Earth in solitude anymore, but I started to withdraw again. The desire to shock myself out of my numbness started catching up with me and I wasn't in a place in my life where I could actually deal with it. I started drinking a lot, going through about a fifth every other day. The smoking didn't help and before long I found myself running away from reality as fast as I could, while somehow functioning and staying somewhat composed on the outside.

I found myself at a crossroads. I didn't want to leave my previous life behind but I was always down for a new adventure. I wasn't ready to settle down by any means. However, I was eager to prove my big heart and the love that I had to share. My past was about to become a distant star, and my unborn girl would soon become my entire world. I wanted to establish a healthy and stable place for our daughter to be brought into, but there was a fracture between Nikki's Washington family and myself. So we moved to Ohio to find support from friends and family.

I had left behind everything and everyone that I loved in order to start fresh and to be a great father and spouse. I knew what I had to do and I took a giant leap in doing so. It was the first time in my life that I had committed to a future that involved more than just myself. The last thing that I ever wanted to do was move to Ohio, but I did it for the right reasons. Although I still don't care for this state much, I'd never take back the sacrifices I made in coming here.

• • •

Everything started out great, and I did what I was supposed to do as a responsible father-to-be. We stayed at her grandparent's house while they were off being snowbirds down in Florida. Their house became our own home base until we could make something happen for ourselves. I quit drinking hard alcohol altogether and cut way back on my smoking, only partaking in moderation from time to time. I got a steady job within a week or so and things seemed to be moving in a good direction. I knew that I had to get my shit all the way together before the baby was born, and so I did. I tried to quit doing everything in my life that could ever be a potential threat to my daughter. The biggest problem in doing so, however, would prove to be a disaster because I had forgotten about taking care of myself in the process.

At this time in my life, work had to be more important than ever. I had to work to provide for my family and make sure that we were going to be okay. So that's what I did. My life now revolved around working and my new little family. The downfall was that I had given up all of my other outlets, positive and negative alike, in order to stay focused.

I couldn't risk getting hurt and not being able to work, so I had to quit skateboarding. There was no photography, art, or music going on anymore. My only outlet became work and loving my girls. It was great, but it was unsustainable and I could only maintain it for so long. Losing skateboarding in my life was like another death blow for me and, as I've established, I wasn't great at coping with loss. It truly was skate or die for me.

I ignored everything that was going on within myself internally and just focused on being a father. Keaura Marie was born on her great grandpa's birthday in May of 2014, which was an amazing day for everyone. She had skis for feet and started out with her daddy's eyes, although they changed to a beautiful brown like her mother's later on. Keaura was the best thing that ever happened in my life and still is the most amazing part of it. Her presence has allowed me to live outside of myself and to use the full potential of my big heart. She unknowingly taught me so much about myself and brought to light new levels of my character that

I never knew existed. As chaotic and stressful as it was to be a new parent raising such a fragile lifeform, it all became worth it with only a simple smile from her beautiful face.

While I was immersed in my work, I had also tasked myself with the resurrection of Nikki's dad's house on the other end of town. He had left it neglected and falling apart, pretty much abandoning it. So I began spending all of my extra time, effort, and money remodeling and fixing up the entire house, virtually on my own. During this time, I had not only changed jobs once but I also was able to start my own business with the help of a partner. It was a rough grind to get started, and I was beginning to spread myself thin between all my endeavors and trying to be a family man but the hard work paid off. I knew that I couldn't drink hard liquor but I soon became comfortable drinking tons of beer. I wouldn't really get drunk, but I was always drinking. I worked my ass off and felt successful, so I felt that I had earned it. As busy as I had become, I never noticed how quickly the garden was growing within.

After a few long months from the time Keaura was born we were able to move into the house that I had worked so hard on. It felt good to finally be our own little family under our own roof. We regularly hosted family in our home, step-brother-in-laws, uncles, grandparents, moms. It seemed normal, but it did cause problems in our relationship because Nikki and I never had enough time of our own together and, if I wasn't working, I was spending time with Keaura. At times, I felt that Nikki was jealous of my relationship with our daughter. I just thought that I was doing the right thing by staying busy, providing for my family, and being a good dad.

Overall, we were doing really well with what we had been given to work with. I loved my girls and I felt like I was doing a good job at showing that, while still trying to pursue my career goals, I could also find balance within our relationships and social lives. I was never the one to know what a healthy relationship should be entirely composed of, but I felt like Nikki and I had that. She was great to me in every way, and she knew how much our daughter meant to me. I knew that neither one of us had intentions to stay in Ohio, and I especially didn't want to be there, so I got tunnel vision in just trying to work my way through. I became preoccupied with dreams of the future instead of concentrating on the amazing things that were right in front of me.

• • •

Successfully accomplishing this fresh start for our new family proved to be fruitful in an unexpected way. Although there were blossoms of happiness, trust, responsibility, accomplishment, and of course love, the fruits being produced were rotten in the core. Anyone in their right mind would have been completely grateful and at peace with anything close to what we had at that time. As good as it seemed and as much as I really wanted it all to work, I can see now that something was definitely missing. It's not that I intended to take my situation for granted. I wasn't consciously trying to be selfish or greedy at all. But there was a part of me that was always thirsty for more, or at least something else. Maybe I had spent so much time being content with the darkness, that I actually feared the light. I was afraid of happiness and success because I didn't want to have it taken away from me. Because of this, I was never truly comfortable with where I was at in life. I was too focused to acknowledge any of this, however. I didn't realize that anything was going awry until I started to quench that thirst with the wrong things.

In trying to leave behind all of the bad, I had accidentally left behind most of the things that were truly mine, things that made me happy. Within me, there was a void that needed to be filled. I was planted right in the middle of an opioid epidemic, and I knew myself too well to get involved. The abundance of pain pills, however, got my attention. As disciplined and as aware as I was about using, these little pills seemed harmless, even something that could fill the void. What could go wrong?

My drinking was becoming a noticeable problem again, but I didn't really care what anyone else thought, as long as I was presentable and functioning as a business owner. Nikki was the only person whose opinion mattered to me, and eventually she herself expressed concern, but tolerated it because of how hard I worked. Eventually, the drinking started to affect my work as well though. Using a couple pain pills a day allowed me to avoid the risk of smelling like alcohol throughout the day, reduce any aches or pains in my body, and have enough energy to be with my family at the end of the work day. A person can only work 12+ hours a day, everyday, for so long before needing some kind of help. It was never about just wanting to get high. It was more about just feeling good enough to be present for all of the hours in the day.

I wasn't afraid of any possible consequences and so I let it become a routine. I was making great money with my business taking off, paying the bills in advance and investing several thousand dollars into new tools. My tunnel vision with work kept me from doing good things with the money. Instead of paying off student loans, taking the girls on vacation, getting tattoos, or even saving for Keaura's future, I started spending all of this extra money on dumb shit. Scratch off tickets, beer, cigs, gas, food, and yes, pills.

It became a habit to just buy pills whenever I had the chance. I had the money, why not? I started to even get some kind of excitement or thrill from just the process of trying to get the pills themselves. Sometimes I would buy quite a few just to have them. But the more that I had on hand, the more that I would use. I eventually enjoyed the buzz that I could get on top of the other benefits, and so I would use more after the normal dose for work purposes, and started getting high. There was even a period of time where I was consistently snorting 8-10 oxycodone 30mg per day, on top of the beer drinking. With the pills, I could maintain my composure working and communicating with our clients. But this eventually became a problem as well, because I would show up late or leave early in order to get my fix. I started feeling guilty for being high at home with the girls, and so I spent more time away. I still felt like I could function and fulfil my responsibilities, but that quickly changed.

• • •

When I realized that the pills were becoming a problem, in more than just a couple of ways, I tried to quit. I've always considered myself to be a strong-willed person, but this was ridiculous. After my body acclimated to doing so many pills over several months, I had become chemically dependent. Going even one day without was pure agony. I would try to drink my way through it in order to function, but even that didn't work. I couldn't go to sleep at night, so I would sleep in the mornings when I was supposed to be up and going to work. I felt like complete shit from the inside out. My bones ached. I was weak. My brain even seemed not to want to function. I became irritated, and began having temperamental mood swings. I had never felt this way in my entire life. Not even a bad case of alcohol poisoning could compare to these withdrawals.

Had it been something that only lasted 2–3 days, I might have made it out. Unfortunately, I had maintained such a busy work schedule and just always being productive, I knew I couldn't risk being out for more than a day or two. Being sick would raise alarms. I couldn't risk being exposed by detoxing for a week or even two, and I certainly couldn't stop the level of endless activity that I was maintaining. My brain and body just couldn't match my willpower. I was trapped, to say the least. This is where it became more dangerous than ever. It was no longer about using to enhance my work performance. It was no longer about using to get high. It was about using just to be able to function at all. I was afraid of the withdrawal symptoms for so many reasons, and so my goal became to try to use minimally to stay afloat and avoid being dope sick.

I had wedged myself into the middle of a vicious cycle of having to use to live, and living just to use. From the moment I woke up until the time I drank myself to sleep, I couldn't not think about pills unless I had just gotten my fix. I became comfortable with the daily struggles of trying to use, but I was depressed with the whole situation. I would use to not feel the physical pain and then want to use more to cover up the emotional pain. I slowly lost sight of my moral compass and my values began to trickle away.

The thousands of dollars I had spent maintaining this self destruction finally caught up to me. I could no longer afford to keep up with the habit, but my brain had already been wired to need these pills as a means of survival. I would manipulate job bids to have money back on materials. I started taking out loans and maxing out credit cards. I would do side jobs in secret, and then have to lie about where I was. In a pinch, I even started stealing money from Nikki. I had also jumped into the circus of pawning my tools and getting them back out as I bounced between what I needed for different jobs. Then I started writing bad checks.

People started to notice that I was screwing up. The closest ones to me, however, tried to give me the benefit of the doubt. They didn't necessarily enable me but they wouldn't call me on my bullshit either, or at least I wasn't noticing if they did. Not long into this nightmare, I had finally gotten into trouble for some bad checks and ended up spending a week in jail before my family bailed me out of serious trouble by paying off my debt to quash the charges. I was forced into withdrawal at that time and I was forced to come clean about my addiction to everyone. It was rough, but it felt like a step in the right direction. I felt so low about myself and what I had done during that time, but I was able to quit. I worked on getting myself together, and was clean for nearly three months.

I ended up taking work out of town. It wasn't ideal by any means, but I had already burnt so many bridges that I didn't really have a choice. Trying to dig myself out of the giant hole that I put myself in seemed impossible. I needed to build a ladder but my only tool at the time was just an old shovel. The debt was overwhelming and not being with my girls all week, every week, started tearing me apart. I felt alone. Really alone. How did I manage to go from on top of the world to barely hanging on by a thread? It was baffling to me.

• • •

Sober or not, I just couldn't cope with everything that had led me up to this place in my life. I had never successfully managed to deal with my past, and on top of that, I had added so much more to the problem. I was losing myself again. Although still going through the motions of doing the right things and being sincere in my love and intentions, my inner light was overshadowed by darkness growing within me. My ego was shot and my insecurities started to prevail. I was depressed, away from the only people I had left close to love, I had lost and forgotten any other positive outlet in my life, and I was struggling with trust issues. Working my way back to my family and happiness seemed unattainable. I couldn't deal with myself and the negativity anymore so I started to use again.

I had straddled the line of finding my way out of the dark, overgrown garden's hold but life didn't seem to give me the opportunity to fully escape. Nikki and I's relationship experienced changes. Distance was difficult, but when I was home for the weekend we were much more passionate and appreciative of each other. Once I was finally able to work a few jobs back home things between us began to get worse and I didn't understand why.

The change in our relationship was so confusing to me and I was already an emotional wreck so I began to suspect she was cheating. One day I found some heartbreaking evidence, and whether or not she actually did cheat on me, I felt betrayed. I couldn't bring myself to leave, but staying also felt wrong. I messed up my job and

Nikki eventually kicked me out of the house because of how addiction affected my behavior. She even started to keep me from seeing my daughter and I just couldn't stand the feeling of despair any longer. At that point, I was hoping for rock bottom so I could climb back up, but the pit seemed to be endless. I just gave up.

Living out of my truck with no place to go, no family within thousands of miles to turn to, and no job. I was screwed. I did everything that I could think of for money to get by, but ultimately I did my best to stay drunk or high, while keeping some gas in the tank. The only places that I could go, or people that I could turn to, were the ones that had been fueling my addiction all along. It seemed as though I was set up for nothing but failure.

Eventually, I managed to secure an opportunity for a job on a tow barge. It wasn't particularly what I wanted but it was certainly what I needed. Room and board, 2-3 weeks out at a time, good money, and more importantly an escape from all of the chaos I had created. It was the perfect chance for me to get back on my feet and headed in the right direction. I had a good inside reference and was well on my way to becoming a deckhand.

Right when this opportunity seemed like an answer to my problems, everything came crashing down again. In one of my not so bright moments, I decided to "borrow" some things, without permission, to pawn so I could get by while waiting on my fresh start. The plan was to return what I could before the people got back from Florida and no one would be the wiser. My logic led me to be indicted on a 2nd degree felony for burglary, which carried a sentence of 2–8 years. My daughter would be three times her age when I got out. In order to demonstrate my remorse, accept responsibility, and hold myself accountable, I pled guilty. After negotiating with the prosecution, I managed to amend my plea agreement, and was resentenced to four years with early release after three.

My daughter would still be twice her age when I got out. This inspired the same kind of emotional break that Brice's death had, and I went emotionally numb again. I had lost everything in my life . . . absolutely everything. I remember thinking that if I only had the chance to just go stay in the woods for even a month, to reground myself, I would never have gotten to this point in my life. I had completely forgotten who I was as a person.

• • •

Being in prison isn't anything like I ever expected. The stereotype of prison we get from movies and stories isn't true. How a person carries themselves, and what choices they make is what really affects the experience. If you are doing sketchy shit with shady people, you are probably asking for trouble. If you just stay in your own lane and focus on doing what you have to do to get back to your family, you most likely won't have any problems. Same as in the real world. There is still a lot going on in prison to keep a person from doing good in here. Drugs, gangs, extortion, thieves, dealing with arrogant C.O.s, and being forced to live with fiends, idiots, and child molesters. Not everyone is a bad person though, far from it. But it does get discouraging.

Upon settling into the fact that I probably wouldn't see Keuara again until she was twice her age, I made the decision to do what was right by my daughter and Nikki. Even just the thought of my daughter's smile gave me the encouragement that I need to know that everything will be fine someday. But more importantly,I had to do this for myself. I had to figure out my problems and fix myself first, because as much as I want to get back to her sooner than later, it wouldn't be right to bring her back a broken father. I started signing up for every program that I could take. Programs like Living Values, House of Healing, Responsible Family Life Skills, Life Without a Crutch, Cage Your Rage, and Thinking for a Change, to name a few. These programs teach you how to deal with issues that involve addiction, character values, anger management, and even coping with prison in a way to find inner peace.

A lot of people were taking these same classes and yet they weren't there for the right reasons. I noticed a pattern that a large majority of the people taking programs were only doing it to look good on their record for the judge. Most of them didn't seem to be applying themselves at all in order to learn or try to change. It really took away from the learning experience for me. While taking these first few programs I was still trying to figure out my way in prison, and although I did pay attention and actually care, I kind of just floated through keeping to myself. The first year of my sentence was a rollercoaster ride of ups and downs. I was still trying to figure out how I got here and to actually accept where I was.

I sometimes catch myself being really jealous in here. All these people running around getting high as fuck and getting tattoos. But the thing is, from my clean and sober perspective now, I get it. Losing absolutely everything in my life and knowing that I am stuck here for years, makes me want to get high more than ever. But that is exactly what put me here to begin with. Breaking the rules had ripped me from Keaura's life, so why would I ever continue to do that? Why would I ever risk doing anything that could postpone me getting back to her? I have to continue to do the right thing every single day, because whether or not anyone sees or cares, it matters.

Passing time in prison is about routine. If you try to do roughly the same thing every single day, more or less, the days eventually blend together and seem to fly by. But it becomes very easy to get complacent, stagnant, or lazy in doing so. There has to be some kind of balance in staying proactive and having some kind of hope and motivation to keep moving forward. My main motivating factor, as I've said, that helps me get through every single day, is my daughter. Even just the thought of her smile gives me the encouragement that I need to know that everything will be fine someday. But in taking a step back, I realized that

I couldn't just do this for her. I had to do this for myself. I had to figure out my problems and fix myself first, because as much as I want to get back to her sooner than later, it wouldn't be right to bring her back a broken father. If I can't be there for myself first, how can I ever be there for her when she needs me?

So I dove into my recovery harder. The more things that stacked against me, the harder I pushed to do the right thing to get through. It hasn't been easy. I see these people running around putting cut up pieces of suboxone strips in their eyes, wondering if that's how crazy I looked in my own addiction. Seeing all the lying, stealing, manipulation, and chaotic behavior, knowing I was that bad at one point, really helped me understand and empathize with the people that I have hurt. Continuing to take different programs and putting more and more clean time under my belt, I am finally starting to see the bigger picture again.

• • •

To this date, I've successfully completed over eighteen programs, and have nearly 30 certificates to prove my progress and accomplishments. I've even completed the one year long Therapeutic Community Program, where we all live together in the same dorm and attend classes all day, all week, all month, the entire year. This excludes weekends and holidays, but we were still held accountable to follow the extensive structure and rules of the program at all times. It was challenging to say the least. Some of the things that I learned were not only identifying and working through my own problems, finding solutions, coping strategies, and even some inner peace, but also that it is incredibly important to communicate effectively and to practice that by giving back to try to help others as well.

In accomplishing all of these programs, I feel good. I actually chose to do the right thing, for the right reasons. Although most of this was all stuff that I knew in my heart, obviously I had lost track of it, so it was good to be refreshed. I feel that it is very important to remember our core and character values in life, and it is surprising to me how easy it can become to lose sight of those things. Learning that addiction really is a disease helped me understand and even somewhat forgive myself.

I had to really dig to discover that my own addiction stemmed from some very faulty coping mechanisms to life's struggles. When Brice died, I shut out the world and sought quick fixes to try to escape the pain rather than facing it head on. I can now admit that was a cowardly thing to do. I took the "easy" way out. I've since learned that although it takes tremendous bravery to stand strong and confront our fears. Reflecting on this now, I'm starting to learn how to forgive myself.

• • •

My grandfather passed away about two years into my sentence. At one point, he was the most important person in my life and I often couldn't fathom how I would react to losing him, especially knowing how hard it was to deal with Brice's passing. I absolutely dreaded the thought of losing him while I was locked up, and I felt ashamed for even putting us in this position. When I got the news on the phone the day after it happened, I knew that I couldn't escape it. I knew I had to use what I had learned, or this vicious cycle of darkness would consume me yet again.

I didn't seek any distractions or try to run from the truth. I allowed the reality of it all to sink in. I reminded myself that death is a natural part of life and that I had to embrace the positive in it. Holding this inside wouldn't help me or anyone else work through this. I reached out to family, doing my best to remind them of grandpa's character and sharing good memories with them. Celebrating his life rather than dwelling on his death seemed to really take the weight off of the loss. Of course it hurt, of course I was devastated, but sometimes a forest must burn in order to make room for new growth.

I even took the initiative to confide in a friend who, it turns out, had experienced a similar loss. This helped me realize that all of us go through forms of loss and tragedy in life, and that self-loathing isn't the way to heal. Actually, opening up to talk about things allowed me to stay included in life. I discovered that, although we may be by ourselves at times, we are truly never alone.

Instead of seeking refuge in substances, negative behaviors, and allowing ourselves to wallow in the darkness, we have the choice to overcome these hard times in life. For some reason, humans tend to live their lives with the perception that bad things only happen to other people. Other people endure sickness, disease, accidents, and die young. Not us. Not the people close to us. Unfortunately, that isn't the case. However, we cannot live in perpetual fear that tragedy is lurking in every shadow either. We must be mindful of the ups and downs that are intrinsically a part of life in order to carry ourselves through.

In finding that balance, we have to remain present and aware. If, *when*, something awful happens, we must deal with it. Talk to someone about it. Concentrate on the good and the ways in which we can honor that loss. Whether it be by focusing those emotions into creative expressions through art, music, and dance, or simply by blowing off some of that energy by working out. For me, I have found relief through writing this zine and, of course, skating. Meditation also does wonders. Believe me, it works. Bottling things up will only lead to an inevitable implosion.

By reflecting on the good times I shared with my grandfather, I was able to find ways to honor his memory. With Brice, it was a shared love of art and skateboarding. However, I was always too fucked up and withdrawn to properly celebrate these shared passions in a way that was therapeutic for me. With my grandfather, it was a shared love of food, playing cards, and road trips. As a kid

I couldn't stand how he would always put pickles on our tuna sandwiches. Now, I make sure to always add one in his memory. It's a small thing, but it is a way in which I can recognize and celebrate his influence on my life. And I look forward to taking my daughter on road trips like the ones that I shared with him.

I've not only learned new coping skills, but have also rediscovered which ones I already had. Skateboarding, art, photography, music, and writing to name a few. It's amazing how much you can grow as a person from simply just writing stuff down on paper. Yes, it is somewhat discouraging doing it all by hand, but it really does help to get it all out on paper and to be able to actually see it. You should try it.

In finding myself again and remembering who Devan actually is as a person, I've been able to reconnect with life and get back on track. I am humble, grateful for all of the little things in life, and am now more confident than ever. I have found my purpose again in moving forward, and have gained much hope through a positive and optimistic attitude. I can say that I really don't know how this journey would have turned out if I didn't have Keaura, so I am thankful for her influence in my decisions and actions to do right. I have realigned my priorities and goals in life. I have made realistic plans to achieve these goals. I have rediscovered the many core and character values that I possess and believe in, and am mindful of using them now. I've learned a lot about myself, about recovery, and I have rebuilt my self worth in the process.

I've learned how to better manage various relationships in my life, and I've really worked on my communication skills. I can say that my biggest problem in struggling through the darkness of my past was absolutely my lack of good communication. Being able to assertively express my thoughts and feelings while keeping a balanced conversation and being an active listener, has been key in my journey to change.

Communication, as I have learned, is composed of 60% body language, 30% tones, and only 10% of the words we actually use. It's no wonder that I have been so lost and misunderstood in the past. Even when I was sincerely saying what I meant, my passive-aggressive tone, lack of eye contact, and closed off posture kept me from fully expressing myself properly. The fact that I was often caught up in my own internal dialogue kept me from fully listening as well.

In order to get the most out of a conversation it is necessary to be an active listener. We often miss out on what the other person is trying to say because we are too preoccupied with what we are going to say next. If we actually take the time to hear what they are saying, paying attention to not only the words but also allowing ourselves to read their body language and understand their tone, we get so much more from the conversation. When we practice being aware of other's body language and tone, it helps us to identify our own as well. It is important to make that healthy eye contact and to have an open and receptive posture. This allows everyone to be more comfortable and engaged.

Active listening also involves *showing* the other person that you are listening. You can do this by briefly summarizing or repeating back what they are saying, using simple phrases like "so it is my understanding that . . .," "so what you're saying is . . .," we not only build confidence in that person by acknowledging that we've heard what they said, but we are also ensuring that both individuals in the conversation understand each other. Without that understanding, we may as well be talking to ourselves.

For so many years I rejected these concepts, but learning how to effectively communicate with other people has taught me how to be more open minded and attentive of those around me. We all use different languages to communicate and those languages reflect the way in which we think and how we go about trying to decipher the world around us. In recognizing that, I have been able to communicate and understand myself better as well. These techniques have given me the ability to better cope with the darkness of that overgrown garden inside. Now I can face the garden head on and allow myself to till my way back into finding some light.

• • •

So, where do I go from here? I've tended to my garden, although I will always have to watch it closely, weeding and pruning between the rows. I now have the tools to maintain it, but I will always have to be mindful of its presence.

In the past, I've allowed myself to be easily swayed or even pushed around by society. I know now that I need to stand my ground and do what's right by me, my beliefs, and the people that I love. I need to stay focused on the path that I know is right while being aware enough to prevent myself from getting tunnel vision or getting off track again.

I deserve to do good things in life. We all do. We need to allow ourselves time for our hobbies and our passions. For me, it is photography, art, driving, music, and most importantly, skateboarding. Rather than isolating, I need to share my love of being adventurous and spontaneous with the people that I care about. The people that we love deserve to have us around. Life is too fragile and short not to just live it and find happiness in sharing it with others.

To me, it all boils down to having the power of choice. Do I want to sit back and let this magnificent chaos of life just swallow me up and pass me by, or do I want to take control of my own small part in it and actually live? I've been given the opportunity to start completely over from scratch. I have absolutely nothing to lose, and everything to gain from here on out. I have no fear of failure at this point, but if I can't choose to overcome my fear of success, I won't go anywhere. I know that I have tremendous potential, and from this second on, I choose to work hard at fulfilling that.

One thing that I've come to understand about my garden is that, whether it be good or bad, darkness or light, what I harvest can be fruitful and yielding once I learn how to use it. Of course, it took me far too long to actually figure this out and understand how to do it. It ultimately boils down to being mindful of oneself. If you can understand your own feelings and thoughts, and know where they come from, you can establish healthy boundaries, take life in moderation, and ultimately find balance within yourself.

We all endure different forms of loss and tragedy throughout our lives. The part that will make or break us is learning how to go about coping with these things. Everybody has their own way that works for them. The bottom line, I believe, is that we have to accept what life throws at us and find some kind of peace with it all in order to move on and continue to grow.

AFTERWORD

My choice to find that peace has brought me to write this story down to share with y'all. If you can take anything away from reading this, I hope that it can at least be some motivation to start chasing your own dreams now. Don't let all the opportunities of life pass you by. We can all start fresh from a clean slate, if we make the choice to do so.

In trying to explain part of my story, and part of my journey through this life, I hope that I've given at least the smallest bit of insight to people that are struggling with similar things. I hope that in explaining the path that led me here, the people in my life that were affected can somewhat understand me now. It's so easy to get caught up in the darkness and to make mistakes and poor choices. Dealing with addiction on top of that multiplies our chances of screwing up so much more. That's not an excuse by any means, don't get me wrong. But it is a fact.

In case this may be my only opportunity to ever apologize, although I intend to make amends and do so in person if possible, I want to say that I am sorry. I am sorry to all the people that have ever been affected by the decisions or actions that I made in the process of struggling with my darkness. Whether you were directly affected by my chaos or indirectly affected by the shockwaves, I'm sorry. I never intentionally wanted to hurt anyone. Forgiveness is for the person that grants it. That being said, I can accept whether you forgive me or not, but I do hope that you can find that within yourselves in order to obtain the peace that you deserve. If so, I sincerely thank you for that.

I mostly want to apologize to my family, friends, and absolutely my girls. Nikki, I know that you have chosen to move on with your life, and I respect that. I want you to know that I love you though, and I always will. Please know that I never meant to hurt you, and I am truly sorry for all the hard times that I imposed on you.

Keaura, your Daddy loves you very much. I want you to know that I am truly sorry for this time that we've lost together. Watching you grow up from afar has been the hardest lesson of my life, and it is a lesson that I will never forget. Thank you so much for being the light of my life and bringing out the best of me. You will always be the hope that inspires me to do good and do right moving forward in life. Thank you for helping me find my path. Although I can't make up for the time we've lost, I will absolutely do everything in my power to make our future together better than ever.

Knowing now that a person needs to take care of themselves first before ever being able to take care of another, I have the wisdom to do so. I'm sorry that I had to learn all of this the hard way. To all my family, friends, and loved ones, I'm sorry for my mistakes, and I want you to know that I love you all.

It's easy for me to say all of the right things over and over to try to convince people that I have truly changed for the better. In fact, I may never be able to convince some. What I can do though is continue to do what I know is right in my heart, saving my breath, because the inner light will absolutely shine through in my actions.

In the Salish culture, one is often asked " stem a spus?us," which can be translated as "What's in your heart?" Until recently, I never fully understood the depth and significance of this question. To answer it truthfully for the first time, I can finally say . . .

I'm done chasing the sunset now and I look forward to enjoying the sunrise at your side.

- Devan

SPECIAL THANKS

To Sarah and everyone at Microcosm for all of your hard work and this great opportunity to share part of my story. Thank you for making this possible.

To all my family and friends that not only stuck by me on this journey of change, but who were always there for me to support, encourage, and aid me in growing through the many seasons of my life, whether you knew it or not. I could never name you all but thank you for contributing to my life.

Particularly Mom, T.A., Lesli, Dustin, Unc, Grandma, Grandpa, Jan, Kailas & Dani, Brice, Ty ben, Darryl, Kenny, Cody, Chris, Camm, the P-Town crew, Janeva, Angelique, Dan Dwayne, Tim, Brandon, Josh, Sheenah, and the ones that I let get away. And of course, I want to thank Nikki and our beautiful daughter, Keaura Marie.

Your love has made my world a better place and I can only hope to make you proud by reciprocating that. Smile for me.